simple machines

Levers

A Buddy Book
by
SARAH TIECK

ABDO
Publishing Company

VISIT US AT
www.abdopublishing.com

Published by ABDO Publishing Company, 4940 Viking Drive, Edina, Minnesota 55435.

Printed in the United States.

Contributing Editor: Michael P. Goecke
Graphic Design: Maria Hosley
Cover Photograph: Photos.com, Clipart.com
Interior Photographs/Illustrations: Clipart.com, Image 100, Image Source, Photos.com, Stock Byte, TONG RO Image Stock

Special thanks to Fred Heim.

Library of Congress Cataloging-in-Publication Data

Tieck, Sarah, 1976–
     Levers / Sarah Tieck.
         p. cm. — (Simple machines)
     Includes index.
     ISBN-13: 978-1-59679-814-4
     ISBN-10: 1-59679-814-9
     1. Levers—Juvenile literature. 2. Lifting and carrying—Juvenile literature. I. Title. II.
Series: Tieck, Sarah, 1976- Simple machines.

TJ147.T485 2006
621.8—dc22
                                                                              2006010043

Table Of
Contents

What Is a Lever?

Levers are used to turn, lift, or move objects. A lever is a simple machine. A simple machine has few moving parts, sometimes only one.

Simple machines give people a mechanical advantage. This is how levers help make work easier for people.

A lever can help control the movement of a train.

Levers are not the only simple machines. There are six simple machines. These include levers, wedges, pulleys, screws, inclined planes, and wheels and axles.

Sometimes, simple machines work together. Most machines are made up of more than one simple machine. Levers are used in doors, hammers, and seesaws.

simple machines

Inclined Planes
Help move objects.

Levers
Help lift or move objects.

Pulleys
Help move, lift, and lower objects.

Screws
Help lift, lower, and fasten objects.

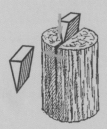

Wedges
Help fasten or split objects.

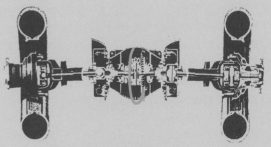

Wheels and Axles
Help move objects.

Parts of A Lever

Levers give people a mechanical advantage. The parts of a lever work together to help move objects. Levers can also help people lift things.

Many parts make a lever work. There is a load. This is the object that needs to be lifted or moved. It supplies resistance.

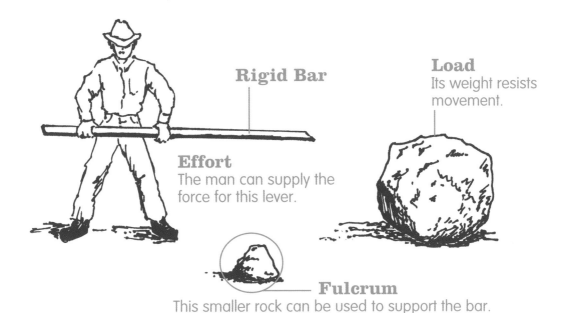

Rigid Bar

Load
Its weight resists movement.

Effort
The man can supply the force for this lever.

Fulcrum
This smaller rock can be used to support the bar.

There is a rigid bar. This helps to position and move the load.

There is a fulcrum. This helps to give support to the bar. Also, this allows the bar to pivot.

Someone or something must supply effort, or force. This is how the load will be turned, lifted, or moved.

How Does A Lever Work?

Most people probably cannot move a heavy load, such as a big rock, alone. But, a person could move a rock with a lever. This is because levers give people a mechanical advantage. This helps make work easier.

To make a lever, the first thing that is needed is a rigid bar. A board or a metal rod would work for this.

Mechanical Advantage
A lever gives a person a mechanical advantage.
The longer the lever, the easier it is to lift the rock.

Next, there needs to be a **fulcrum** to support the board. A smaller rock would work for this.

The **fulcrum** should be positioned near the rock. The closer the fulcrum is to the rock, the easier the rock is to move. The bar will **pivot** on the fulcrum.

The rock is the **resistance**. A person, or another machine provides the **force**. The person should be positioned at the end of the bar farthest from the rock.

To move the rock, a person needs to push down, or apply force, on one end of the bar. This action helps move or lift the rock's weight at the other end.

Different Levers At Work

There are different types of levers. Different levers move in different ways. There are many ways to change how a lever works.

There are three main kinds of levers. These are called the first-class lever, the second-class lever, and the third-class lever.

In a first-class lever, the **fulcrum** is placed between the **resistance** and the **effort**. A seesaw is an example of a first-class lever.

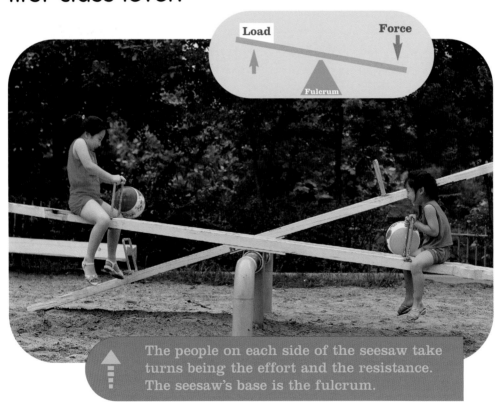

The people on each side of the seesaw take turns being the effort and the resistance. The seesaw's base is the fulcrum.

In a second-class lever, the **resistance** is between the **fulcrum** and the **effort**. A wheelbarrow is an example of a second-class lever.

Load

Force

Fulcrum

The person using the wheelbarrow provides the effort. The load in the wheelbarrow is the resistance. The wheelbarrow's wheel is the fulcrum.

Load

Fulcrum

Force

A person's hands serve as the fulcrum and provide the effort. The resistance is at the end of the bat.

In a third-class lever, the **effort** is between the **fulcrum** and the **resistance**. Using a baseball bat is an example of a third-class lever.

The History of Levers

The lever has been used for many, many years. Some people say a Greek mathematician named Archimedes discovered the lever. Ancient people had probably been using levers for many years, but Archimedes was one of the first to write about this simple machine. This happened around 260 BC.

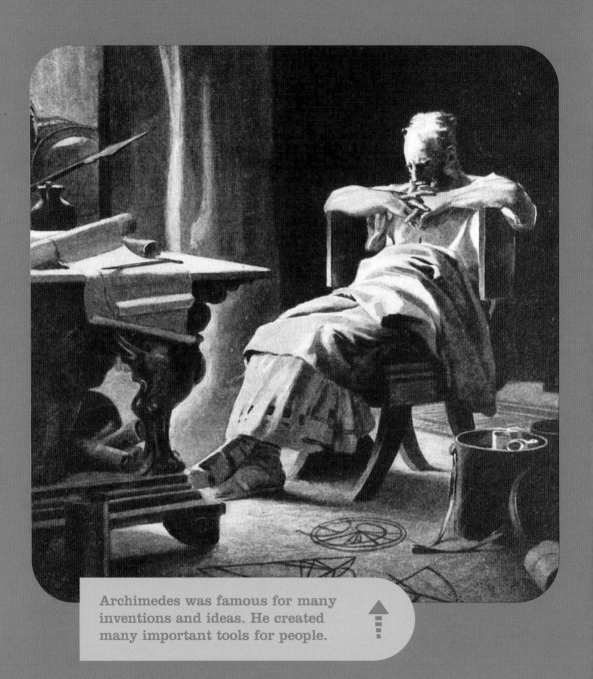

Archimedes was famous for many inventions and ideas. He created many important tools for people.

In Archimedes's time, people didn't have machines with motors. People had to do work with their bodies. Archimedes helped them understand how to use levers to make work easier.

Archimedes was famous for his ideas. He knew a lot about mathematics and science. He was always experimenting with formulas and theories. Many times he discovered tools that helped people. Some of his tools and ideas are still used today.

How Do Levers Help People Today?

Today people have many types of tools. But they still use levers.

When you open a door, you are using a lever. When you sweep the floor with a broom, you are using a lever. When you cut a piece of paper with scissors, you are using another type of lever.

When a person uses a broom to sweep, he or she is using a lever to do work.

A bottle opener *(left)* is a type of lever. So is a pair of scissors *(right)*.

Levers help people with many different jobs all over the world.

Web Sites

To learn more about **Levers**, visit ABDO Publishing Company on the World Wide Web. Web site links about **Levers** are featured on our Book Links page. These links are routinely monitored and updated to provide the most current information available.

www.abdopublishing.com

Important Words

effort an attempt to lift or move something.

force a push or pull against resistance.

fulcrum the support or point on which a lever rests when it is lifting something.

inclined plane a flat surface that is raised at one end. This is a type of simple machine that helps move objects to higher or lower places.

load an object that needs to be turned, lifted, or moved.

mechanical advantage the way simple machines make work easier. Using a simple machine to help with a task means less, or different, effort is needed to do a job. The same job would require more effort without the help of a simple machine.

pivot to move as if fixed to a pin.

resistance something that works against or opposes.

Index